LEARN TO DRAW

DISNEY

Winnie the Pooh

Illustrated by Olga Mosqueda and Marianne Tucker

Walter Foster

1 3 5 7 9 10 8 6 4 2

Table of Contents

The Story of

Disney
Winnie the Pooh

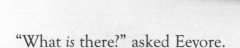

Christopher Robin had lots of toys, but the stuffed animals were his favorites—especially a bear called Winnie the Pooh. The boy and his well-worn friends spent many happy hours sharing make-believe adventures in a place called the Hundred-Acre Wood.

Every night while Pooh slept, he dreamed of honey—his favorite thing. One morning, Pooh woke up to discover there was no honey in his house. He went into the Hundred-Acre Wood to find some more. Pooh came upon Eeyore, the donkey.

"Eeyore," said Pooh. "What has happened to your tail? It isn't there."

"What *is* there?" asked Eeyore.

"Nothing," replied Pooh, who resolved to find it.

Owl suggested promising a prize to anyone who found a replacement tail for Eeyore. "We will have a contest to find a new tail for Eeyore," said Christopher Robin. "The prize shall be a pot of honey!"

Pooh wondered what would make a suitable tail for Eeyore. He dashed home, where the most perfect tail he could think of was hanging on his wall. "Thanks, Pooh," said Eeyore after Pooh outfitted him with a Pooh-koo clock. The friends declared Pooh the contest winner and presented him with a pot

of honey! But before Pooh could scoop out even one pawful, Eeyore sat on his clock tail and crushed it.

"We could give B'loon a try," suggested Piglet. He tied the red balloon to Eeyore's bottom, but Eeyore started to float away.

Christopher Robin pulled Eeyore back and untied the balloon. "Let's try something else," he said. The friends tried many more things, but nothing worked.

"I may have just the thing," said Kanga. She attached her scarf to Eeyore's backside. It worked! But a little while later, Pooh noticed a piece of yarn on the ground. He followed it straight to Eeyore. Kanga's scarf had unraveled!

Later, Pooh went to Christopher Robin's house in search of honey. Christopher Robin was not home, but there was a note on the doorstep. Puzzled, Pooh took the note to Owl's house. Owl said, "It says, 'Gone out, busy Backson. Signed Christopher Robin.' Our friend has been captured by a creature called the Backson!" The friends gasped in fear.

Rabbit came up with a plan. They would collect things that the Backson liked, and leave a trail to lure him into a pit so the Backson would be trapped. Then they could get Christopher Robin back!

Pooh and Piglet chose the location for the pit. When they found the perfect spot, Piglet dug the pit and covered it with a cloth, weighing down its corners with four heavy rocks. Then Piglet put a honeypot on top of the cloth to help disguise the trap.

Meanwhile, Tigger had decided to track the Backson on his own. He was sure he had found him, too, when he pounced on something moving in the Wood. It was Eeyore.

"You and me are going to catch that Backson together!" Tigger declared. "But if you're gonna pounce you got to have some bounce. We need to get you tiggerized!" Tigger gave Eeyore stripes. Then he attached a large spring to the end of Eeyore's tail and set him in motion. The donkey went up and down . . . up and down . . . up and down—and, shortly thereafter, just up. The friends ended up in Rabbit's garden. Tigger dressed up as the Backson and coached Eeyore on how a tigger would "bounce" the monster into surrendering. The poor donkey ricocheted from one place to another and then simply bounced away into the woods. When Tigger

searched for his friend, all he found was Eeyore's springy tail.

Pooh did his best to concentrate on finding Christopher Robin, but his shadow started looking like a honeypot! Then the ground melted into a honey ocean! Pooh swam, dived, and floated in the honey. He gobbled, gulped, and guzzled the honey. Suddenly—POOF!—his daydream disappeared. His honey "ocean" was only a muddy puddle—and Pooh was a great, big mess!

After Pooh cleaned up, he came upon a large honeypot centered in the middle of a cloth. He was so excited that he didn't recognize the Backson trap he and Piglet had set earlier. Pooh fell to the bottom of the pit and the empty honeypot fell on top of his head. Meanwhile, Pooh's friends had arrived at the pit. They heard a loud THUD! The friends clung to each other in fear.

Rabbit exclaimed, "We caught the Backson!"

"Alright, Backson," said Rabbit as the group peered into the pit. "Give us Christopher Robin back."

"Oh, bother," said Pooh, bumping into the walls of the pit.

"Pooh?" asked Rabbit.

"Is that you, Pooh?" asked Piglet.

Just then, Eeyore arrived at the pit and showed off his newest tail. It was an anchor he found in the stream. Rabbit thought Eeyore's anchor tail might help rescue Pooh, so he threw it into the pit. But it was so heavy, it yanked all the friends down into the hole—and broke the honeypot on Pooh's head. Only Piglet, who had been tossed high into the air, remained on the ground.

"Wait for me!" Piglet cried as he started to climb into the pit.

"No, Piglet!" Rabbit cried. "Look for something to get us out!"

Piglet returned with a flower, but it was too short. Next, Piglet brought back a large book, but that didn't work either. On Piglet's third trip, he brought a useful rope. And because there were six friends, Piglet cut the rope into six equal pieces, but they were much too short. Owl flew out of the pit to encourage Piglet to get Christopher Robin's jump rope. Then he flew back in. (Owl did not need rescuing, but no one seemed to notice.)

Piglet trudged nervously into the woods. As he looked around, he backed into a very large tree root. Startled, he turned and saw what looked like a red-eye monster glaring down at him, but it was only B'loon. As Piglet pulled

B'loon from the tree, an enormous shadow fell over him.

"B-B-B-BACKSON!" Piglet shouted. He held on tight to B'loon and raced away. But it was only Tigger dressed in his Backson disguise. But now Tigger thought the Backson was right behind him! He ran after his friend so that they could flee together. "Piglet!" he cried.

"He knows my name!" shrieked Piglet. "Help!"

Piglet spotted the pit in the distance. He had nearly made it when Tigger crashed into him. Down into the pit they both tumbled.

When the dust settled, everyone was relieved to see it was only Tigger. Pooh looked up and saw a honeypot at the edge of the pit. He decided to build himself a letter ladder. The friends all climbed up the ladder and were relieved to be out of the pit—until they heard a rustling in the bushes. "Backson!" they cried. But it was only Christopher Robin.

"How did you escape from the Backson?" asked Rabbit.

"What is a Backson?" Christopher Robin asked.

"The most wretched creature that you could meet," Owl said solemnly.

"What gave you the idea I was taken by a Backson?" said Christopher Robin.

Pooh handed him the note. Christopher Robin giggled. He explained that he had written that he would be "back soon"—not "Backson." It had all been a misunderstanding!

Later, Pooh continued his honey search at Owl's house. He climbed up the tree to Owl's front door, where he pulled the new bell rope. There was something familiar about the rope. As Owl invited Pooh inside he said, "I found that bell rope hanging over a thistle bush. Nobody seemed to want it, so I brought it home."

"But somebody did want it, Owl," Pooh said. "My friend Eeyore. He was attached to it, you see." It was Eeyore's tail!

Pooh took the tail to Christopher Robin, who attached it to Eeyore with a hammer and nail. Eeyore considered his new tail. "Seems about the right length. Pink bow's a nice touch. Swishes real good, too," he said.

"Bring out the grand prize!" Christopher Robin instructed.

"Thank you all ever so much," said Pooh as he climbed into the giant honeypot. All his honey dreams had finally come true!

Tools and Materials

Before you begin drawing, you will need to gather a few tools. Start with a regular pencil, an eraser, and a pencil sharpener. When you're finished with your drawing, you can bring your characters to life by adding color with crayons, colored pencils, markers, or even watercolor or acrylic paints!

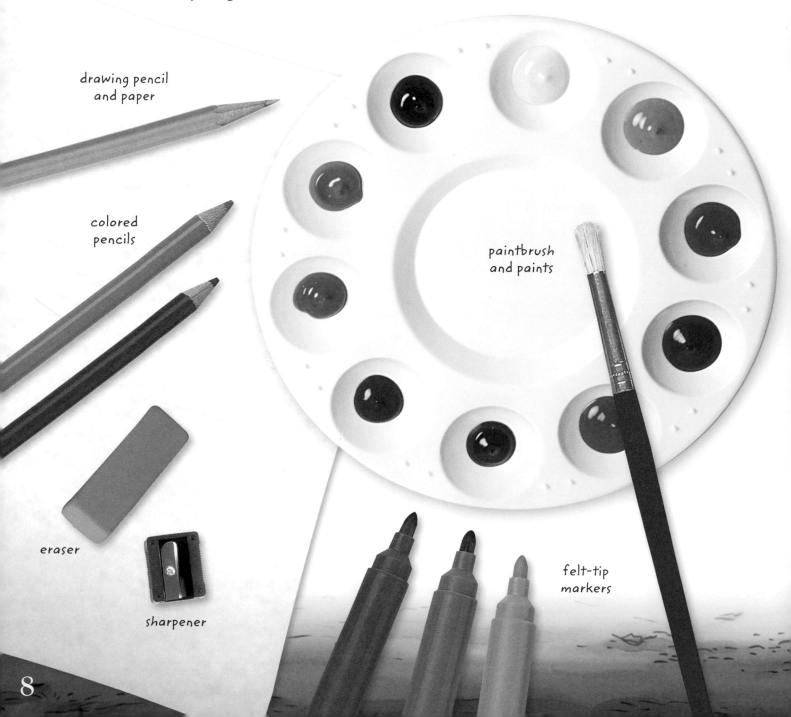

drawing pencil and paper

colored pencils

paintbrush and paints

eraser

sharpener

felt-tip markers

Getting Started

The first thing you'll need is a pencil with a good eraser. Lots of times when artists draw characters, they make extra lines to help them figure out where to put things like noses and ears and whiskers. If you use a pencil, you can erase these lines when your drawing is finished.

First you'll draw guidelines to help position the character's features.

Next, you'll start to add details. It will take several steps to add them all.

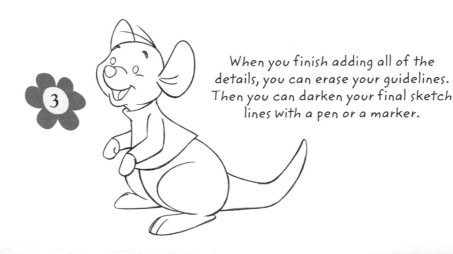

When you finish adding all of the details, you can erase your guidelines. Then you can darken your final sketch lines with a pen or a marker.

Drawing Exercises

Warm up your hand by drawing lots of squiggles and shapes.

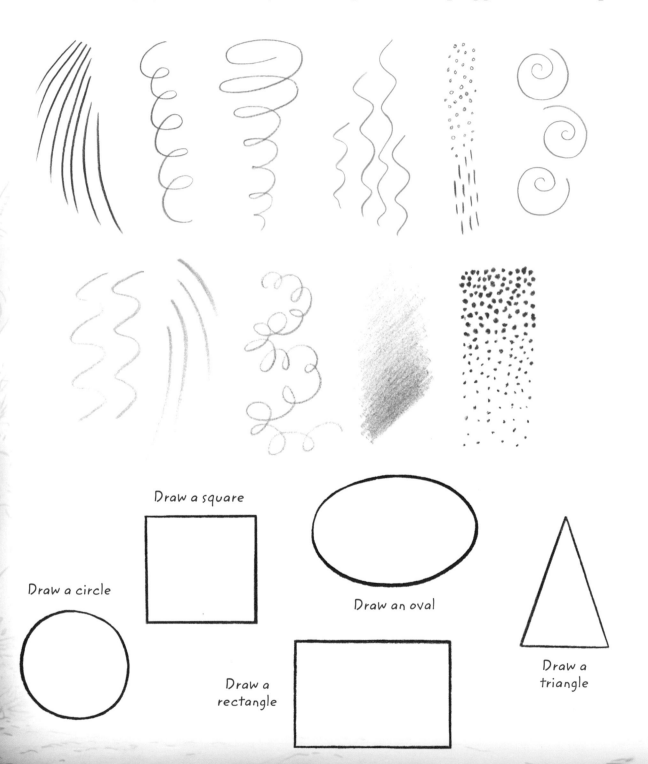

Draw a square

Draw an oval

Draw a circle

Draw a rectangle

Draw a triangle

If you can draw a few basic shapes,
you can draw just about anything!

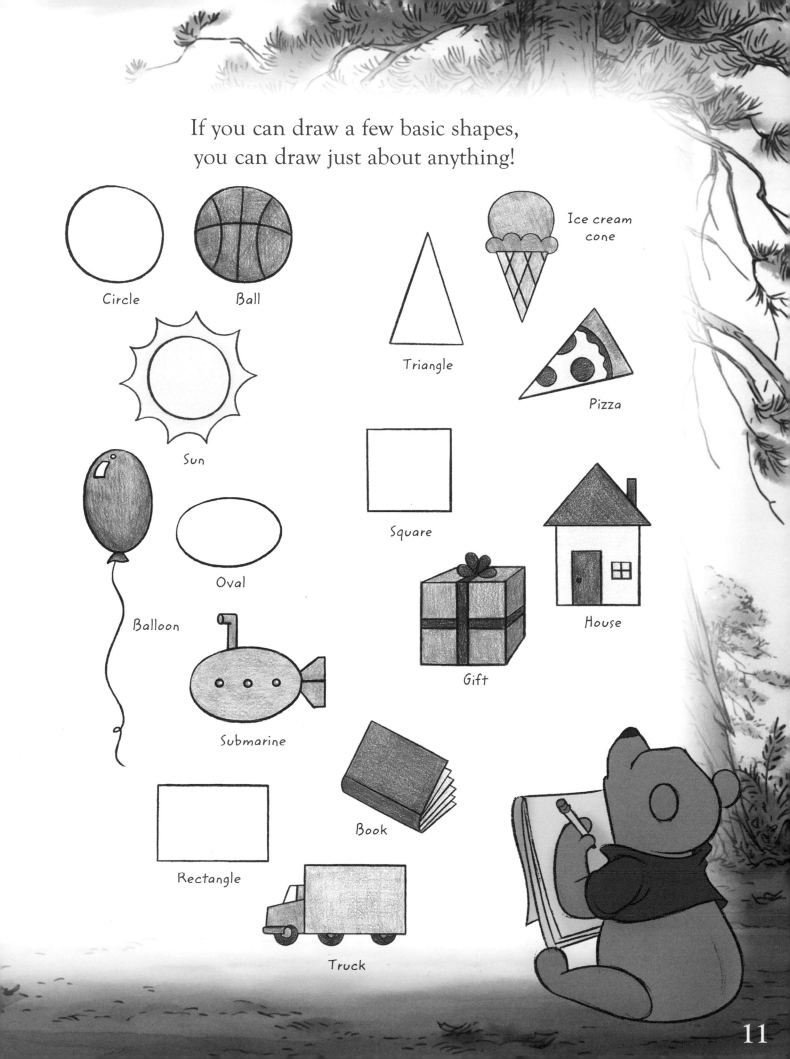

Circle

Ball

Ice cream cone

Triangle

Pizza

Sun

Square

Oval

Balloon

Submarine

Gift

House

Rectangle

Book

Truck

Winnie the Pooh

Pooh is a bear of little brain and big tummy. He has a one-food mind when it comes to honey. But he is also a good friend to Piglet and a perfect pal for "doing nothing" with Christopher Robin. Pooh has a simple sweetness to him that goes beyond the honey stuck to his paws.

Pooh's head is a slightly stretched circle

Pooh's nose is a soft triangle—
not a round circle—
and a little flat on the top

NO!

YES!

4

5

6

7

8

13

Sometimes Disney artists look in the mirror to see how to draw certain expressions. If Pooh were drawing a picture of himself, he'd have a perfect model for a giggling bear!

1

2

Pooh's muzzle is egg-shaped.

3

the bridge of his nose is a soft S shape

he has a smile line at the corner of his mouth

4

Pooh's lip line is just under his muzzle

Pooh's eyebrows are on the soft curve of his forehead

7

8

Pooh's head looks like a circle, and his body looks like a pear. He is about 2-½ heads high, and his toes point in a little. Pooh's shirt is loose fitting, too. Piglet thinks the silly old bear is a wonderful friend.

Pooh's ears are halfway between the top and back of his head

his eyes are set on the muzzle line

3

4

5

6

the length
of Pooh's
arms ends at
the widest
part of his
tummy

Pooh's hands are simple—no fingers, just thumbs

7

8

Tigger

Tigger is one of a kind in the Hundred-Acre Wood. He is always sure of "what tiggers do best," even before he does something. But perhaps the really "wonderful thing" about Tigger is the bounce he brings to everyone around him.

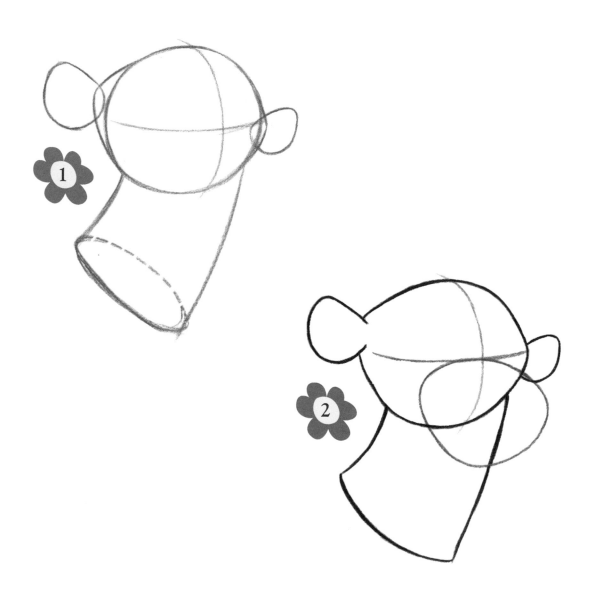

Tigger's head is diamond-shaped and has flat planes on top

YES!

his head is not too round

NO!

23

5

6

Tigger's eyes are small and close together; his nose is triangle-shaped

YES!

NO!

Tigger's head and muzzle are oval-shaped. He often has a big grin on his face, but when his feelings get hurt, his whiskers droop toward the ground.

3

4

YES!
Tigger's nose
is large

NO!
don't make
it too small

the stripe on top of
Tigger's head also serves
as his eyebrows

Tigger's body is kind of shaped like a banana. His arms are longer than his legs, and he has a combination of large and small stripes on his body. Tigger's long tail squishes when he bounces, which is often.

Tigger's tail is
like a spring when
he bounces

when standing or walking, Tigger's tail
is angular, as if a spring is coiled inside

Tigger's hands are like
mittens with no fingers

Piglet

Piglet is a very small animal. He is little enough to be swept away by a leaf and timid enough to be scared by Owl's chilling description of a "Backson." Piglet's eyebrows and mouth usually show how he's feeling.

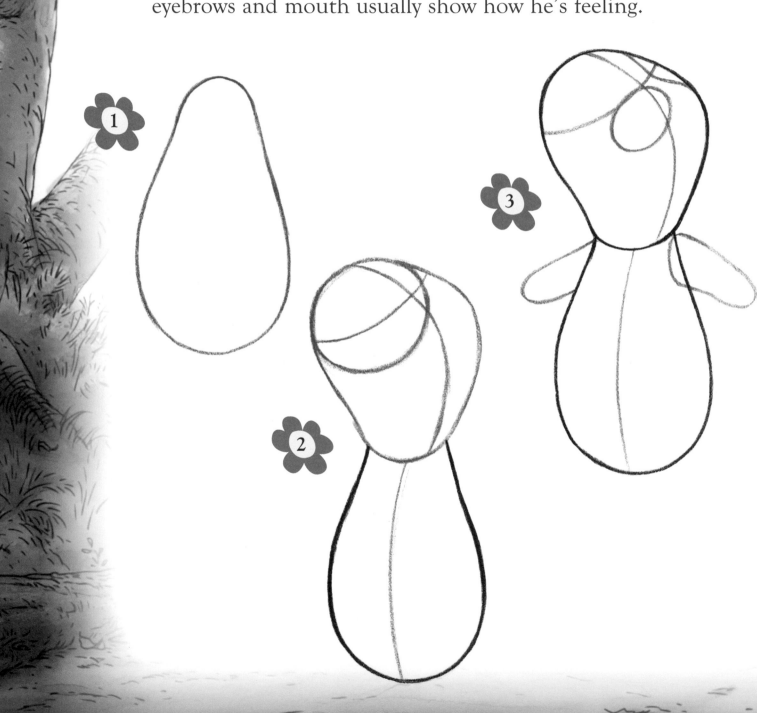

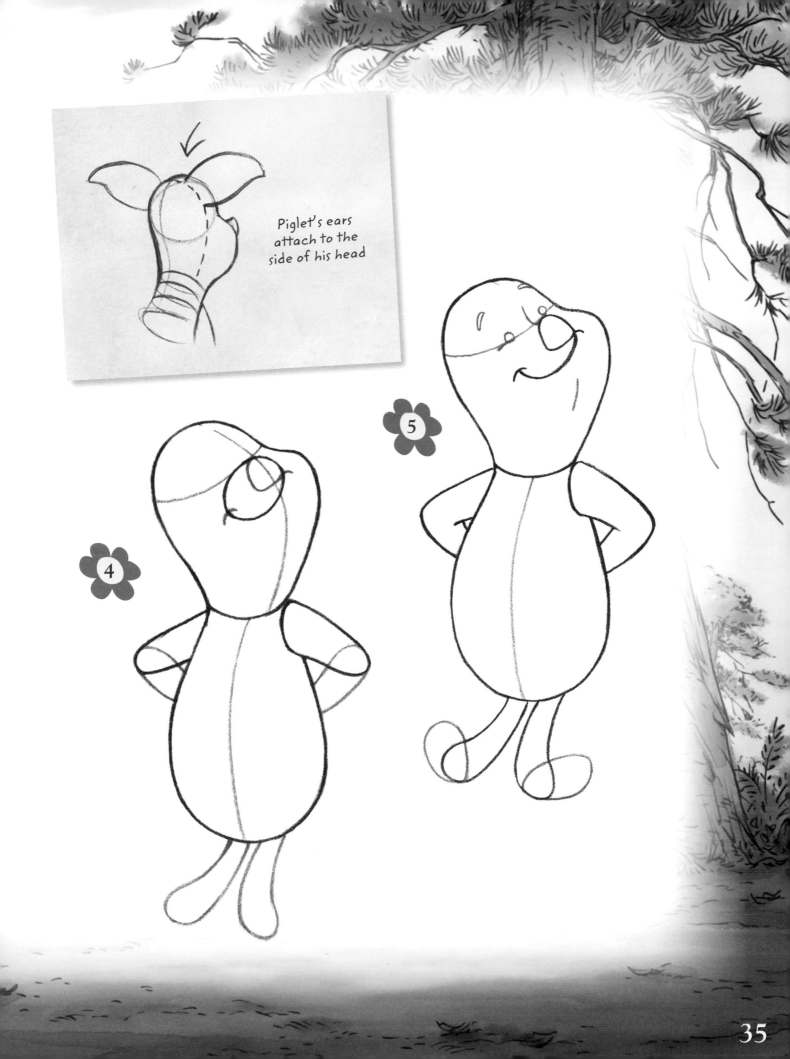

Piglet's ears attach to the side of his head

Piglet's clothing lines should wrap around his body

YES!

round

NO!

flat

6

Eeyore

Things are always looking down for Eeyore. With a tail that comes loose and a house that collapses, he's always ready for things to go wrong. Still, Eeyore manages to smile once in a while, even though he's almost always gloomy.

his ears are long and come to a point

Eeyore's
mane
falls
forward

Poor Eeyore always seems to be losing his tail. He can't even imagine what it must be like to have a springy tail like Tigger's that never falls off—even with the bounciest of bounces.

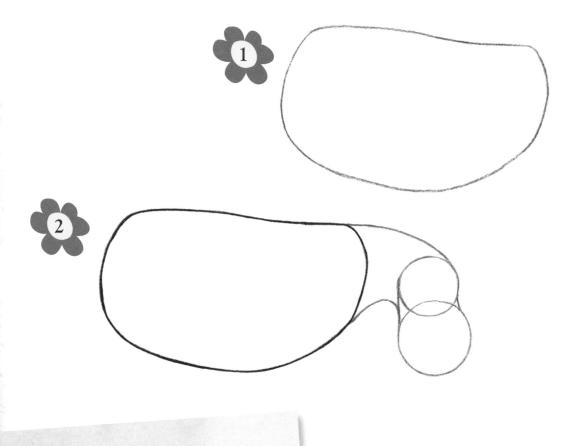

1

2

Eeyore's limbs are soft— remember, he is a stuffed animal

YES!

NO!

his neck and head are just
about the same length

Eeyore's head starts with 2
circles—a small one for the
head and a larger one for
the muzzle

8

Kanga

Kanga is like a mother to everyone in the Hundred-Acre Wood, but especially to her own little one, Roo. She is as sweet and playful as she is protective and concerned—and she cares for all of the animals.

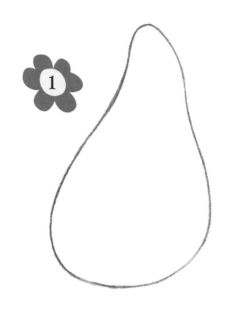

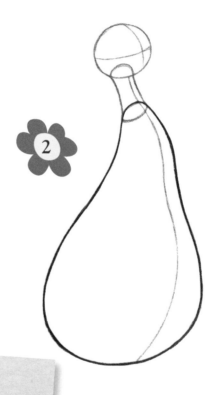

Kanga's body, arms, and legs are soft and round

YES!

NO!

Kanga's ears are as
long as her head

don't make them
too small

Roo

Roo agrees with his best buddy Tigger that bouncing is fun, fun, fun—and he imitates Tigger's bouncing whenever he can. Tigger is like a big brother to Roo, and the two friends just love bouncing from one adventure to the other in the Hundred-Acre Wood.

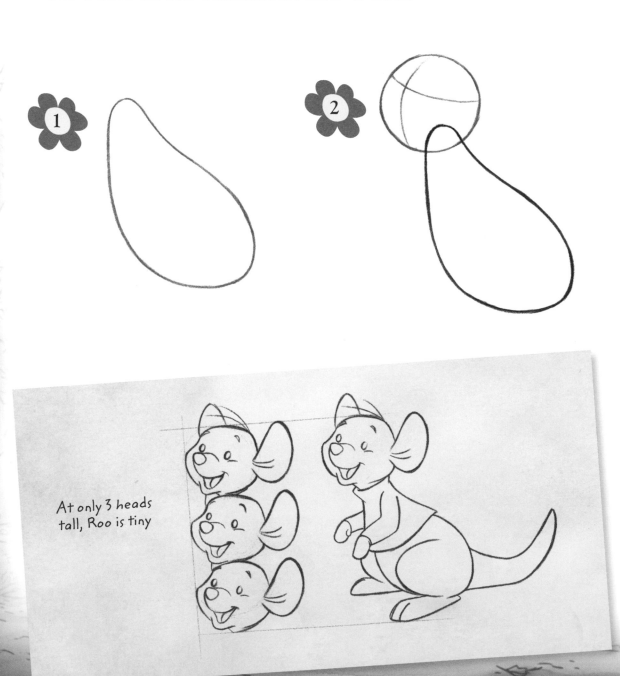

At only 3 heads tall, Roo is tiny

3

Roo's hands and arms are simple—no fingers, just a thumb

4

5

6

Roo's eyes are set wide apart

YES!

NO!

7

Roo's ears are shaped like a kidney bean and are about the same height as his head

8

Rabbit

Rabbit is very organized, right down to the neat rows of vegetables in his garden. He can be fussy and is easily frustrated, but Rabbit is still a good friend to the others. And Pooh and his friends are good friends to him, too.

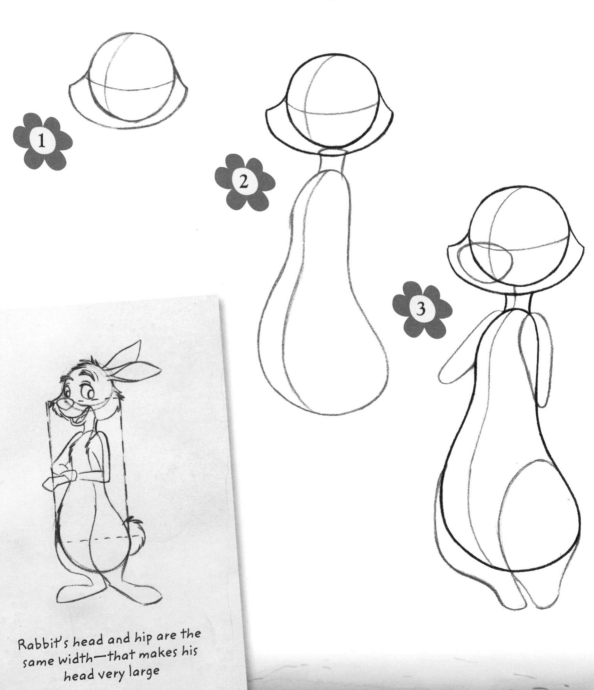

Rabbit's head and hip are the same width—that makes his head very large

Rabbit's feet have 3 toes

6

Rabbit's hands have 3 fingers and a thumb—more human than the other characters

7

Owl

Owl likes to talk. And talk, and talk, and talk. When his friends stop by for a visit, Owl doesn't simply talk about the who. He also likes to talk about the what, where, when, why, and how in lots and lots of detail. Still, Pooh often asks Owl for advice.

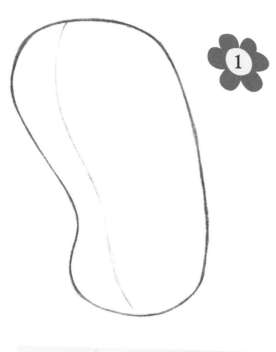

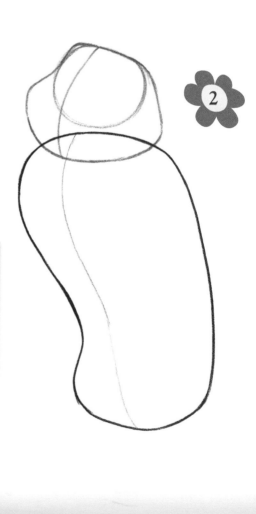

Owl is larger on the top

and smaller on the bottom

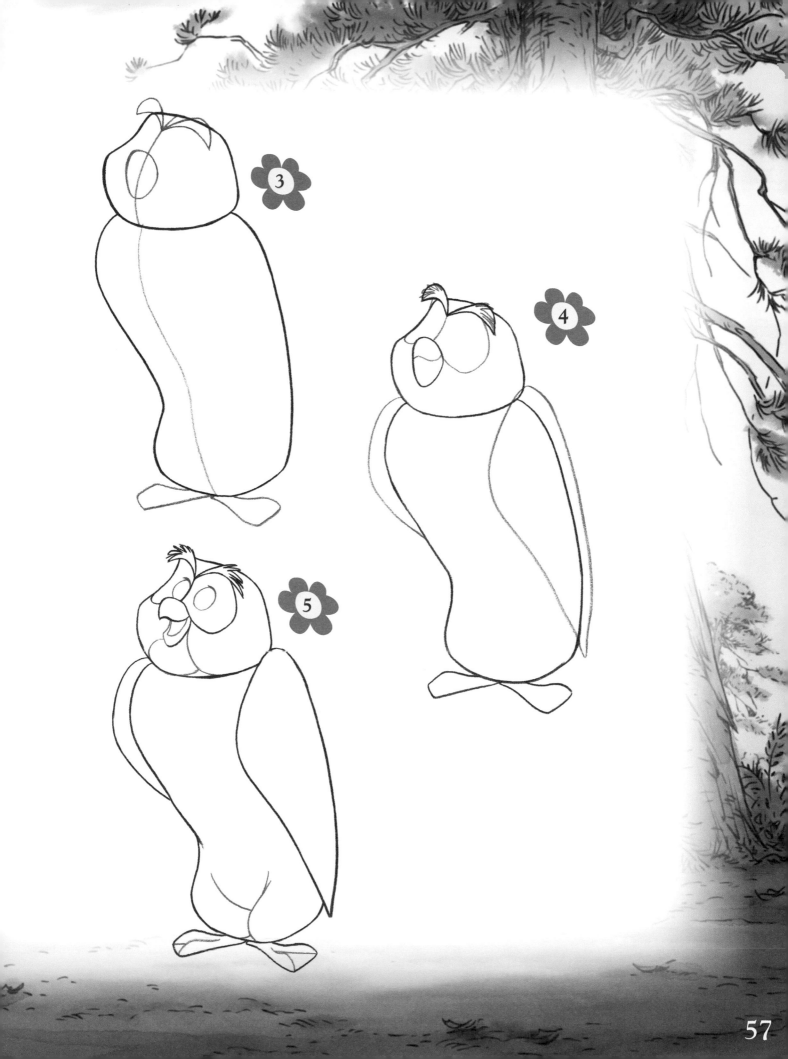

3

4

5

6

NO!   YES!

Owl's eyes are big,
but his beak is small

Owl's wings can open

7

Christopher Robin

Even though Christopher Robin is really a child, Pooh and his friends always come to him for help. Whether Eeyore has lost his tail or Pooh is stuck in Rabbit's doorway, Christopher Robin usually knows how to solve the problem.

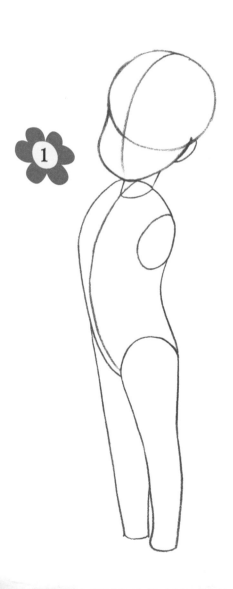

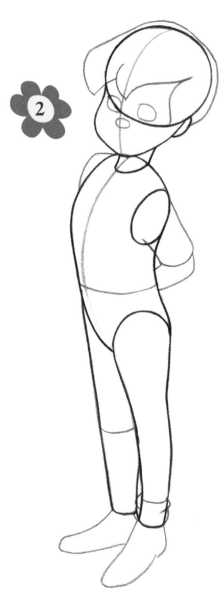

his hair is loose and messy

Christopher Robin's eyes are large and always open wide

Christopher Robin's socks are always at different levels: the right sock is high and under his knee; the left sock is down near his ankle

5 heads tall

5

Nowhere is a wonderful place—
especially when you're beside
your best friend.